WORKING PAPERS

for use with

MANAGERIAL ACCOUNTING

Eighth Edition

Ray H. Garrison
Brigham Young University
Eric W. Noreen
University of Washington

IRWIN

Chicago • Bogotá • Boston • Buenos Aires • Caracas
London • Madrid • Mexico City • Sydney • Toronto

Printed in the United States of America.

ISBN 0–256–16920–9

1 2 3 4 5 6 7 8 9 0 EB 4 3 2 1 0 9 8 7

CONTENTS

1.

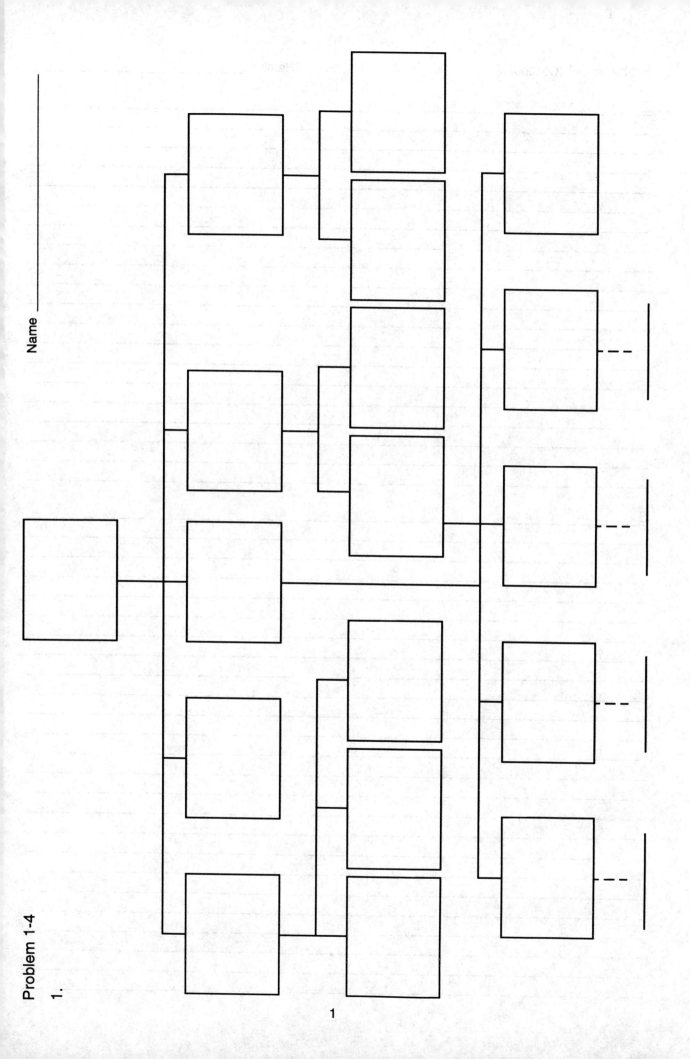

2.

3.

Problem 1-5   Name _____

1. _____

_____

_____

_____

_____

_____

_____

_____

_____

_____

_____

_____

_____

_____

_____

_____

_____

_____

2. _____

_____

_____

_____

_____

_____

_____

_____

_____

_____

_____

_____

_____

_____

_____

_____

_____

_____

_____

_____

_____

1. _____

2. _____

3. a. and b.

Name _____

1. _____

_____

_____

_____

_____

_____

_____

_____

_____

_____

_____

_____

_____

_____

_____

_____

_____

_____

_____

_____

_____

2. _____

_____

_____

_____

_____

_____

_____

_____

_____

_____

_____

_____

_____

_____

_____

_____

_____

_____

_____

_____

_____

_____

3. _____

_____

_____

_____

_____

_____

_____

_____

_____

_____

_____

_____

_____

_____

_____

_____

_____

_____

_____

_____

_____

_____

Name _____

1. _____

2. _____

Name _____

The sketch of the product flow line would be as follows:

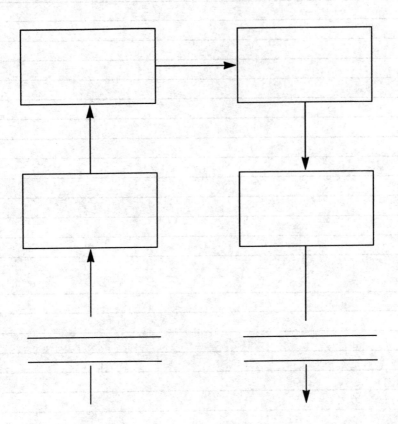

Problem 1-9   Name _____

1. _____

2. _____

Name _____

1. _____

2. _____

Problem 2-10

| Name of the Cost | Variable Cost | Fixed Cost | Product Cost | | | Period (Selling & Admin.) Cost | Opportunity Cost | Sunk Cost |
			Direct Materials	Direct Labor	Mfg. Overhead			

	1	2	3	4

Problem 2-12

Name _____

	1.				

1.

2.

3.

4.

1. _____ MEDCO, INC. _____

2. _____   MEDCO, INC. _____

3.

4.

5.

Problem 2-14

1.

Cost Item	Cost Behavior		Selling or Administrative Cost	Product Cost	
	Variable	Fixed		Direct	Indirect

2.

3.

4. a.

  b.

Name _____

1. _____

2. _____

Problem 2-16

Cost Item	Variable or Fixed	Selling Cost	Administrative Cost	Manufacturing (Product) Cost	
				Direct	Indirect
1.					
2.					
3.					
4.					
5.					
6.					
7.					
8.					
9.					
10.					
11.					
12.					
13.					
14.					
15.					
16.					
17.					
18.					
19.					
20.					

Problem 2-17

1.

Name of the Cost	Variable Cost	Fixed Cost	Product Cost			Period (Selling & Admin.) Cost	Opportunity Cost	Sunk Cost
			Direct Materials	Direct Labor	Mfg. Overhead			

2. _____

1. _____ SKYLER COMPANY _____

2. _____ SKYLER COMPANY _____

3.

1. _____ VALENKO COMPANY _____

2. _____

_____

_____

3. _____

_____

_____

_____

_____

_____

_____

_____

_____

_____

_____

4. _____

_____

_____

_____

_____

_____

_____

_____

_____

_____

_____

_____

_____

_____

_____

_____

_____

_____

_____

_____

_____

Cost Item	Cost Behavior		To Units of Product	
	Variable	Fixed	Direct	Indirect
1. Plastic washers used in auto production				
2. Production superintendent's salary				
3. Laborers assembling a product				
4. Electricity for operation of machines				
5. Janitorial salaries				
6. Clay used in brick production				
7. Rent on factory building				
8. Wood used in ski production				
9. Screws used in furniture production				
10. A supervisor's salary				
11. Cloth used in suit production				
12. Depreciation of cafeteria equipment				
13. Glue used in textbook production				
14. Lubricants for machines				
15. Paper used in textbook production				

1. _____HICKEY COMPANY_____

2. a. _____

b. _____

3. _____ HICKEY COMPANY _____

Problem 3-12   Name _____

1.

a.				
b.				
c.				
d.				
e.				
f.				
g.				
h.				
i.				
j.				

2.

Raw Materials	Manufacturing Overhead

Work in Process	Cost of Goods Sold

Finished Goods

3. _____
_____
_____
_____
_____
_____

4.   RAVSTEN COMPANY

Problem 3-13   Name _____

1. and 2.

Cash	Finished Goods	Salaries and Wages Payable

		Capital Stock

Accounts Receivable	Prepaid Insurance	Retained Earnings

		Sales

Raw Materials	Plant and Equipment	Cost of Goods Sold

		Depreciation Expense

Work in Process	Accumulated Depreciation	Sales Commissions Expense

		Admin. Salaries Expense

Manufacturing Overhead	Accounts Payable	Insurance Expense

		Miscellaneous Expense

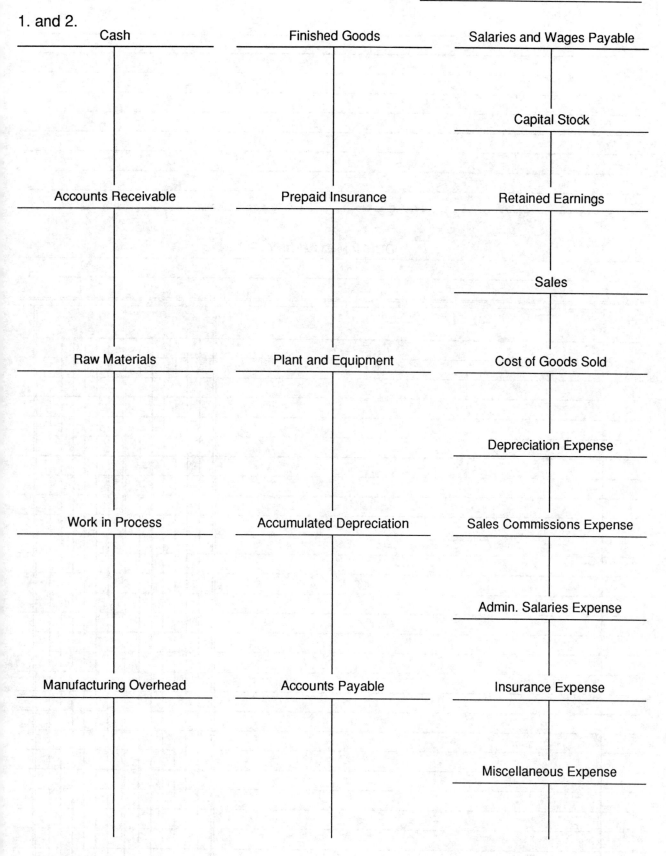

Problem 3-13 (Continued)   Name _____

3.
_____
_____
_____
_____
_____
_____
_____
_____
_____

4.   DURHAM COMPANY
_____
_____

Problem 3-14

Name _____

1. and 2.

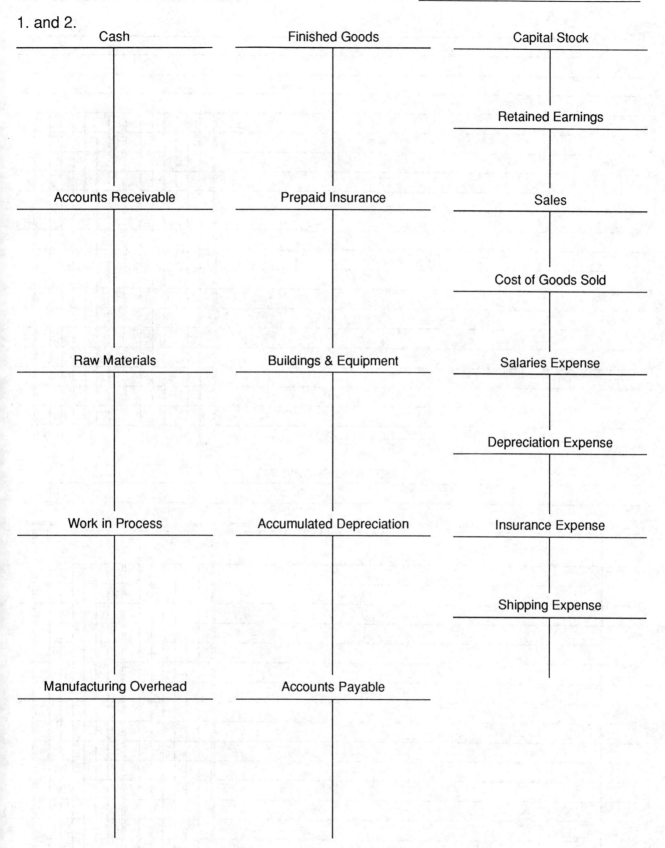

Cash

Accounts Receivable

Raw Materials

Work in Process

Manufacturing Overhead

Finished Goods

Prepaid Insurance

Buildings & Equipment

Accumulated Depreciation

Accounts Payable

Capital Stock

Retained Earnings

Sales

Cost of Goods Sold

Salaries Expense

Depreciation Expense

Insurance Expense

Shipping Expense

3. _____

4. FANTASTIC PROPS, INC.

Problem 3-15   Name _____

1.

a.

b.

c.

d.

e.

f.

g.

h.

i.

j.

2.

Raw Materials	Manufacturing Overhead

Work in Process	Cost of Goods Sold

Finished Goods

3. _____
_____
_____
_____
_____
_____

4. _____ SOVEREIGN MILLWORK, INC. _____
_____

1. a. _____

   b. _____

2.   PACIFIC MANUFACTURING CO.

3.

4.

5.

Problem 3-17

Name _____

1. _____

_____

_____

_____

_____

_____

_____

_____

_____

_____

2. _____

_____

_____

_____

3.

	Dept. A	Dept. B	Total

4.

	Dept. A	Dept. B

Problem 3-18

Name _____

1.

Raw Materials	Work in Process	Finished Goods

Manufacturing Overhead	Salaries & Wages Payable	Accounts Payable

2. a.

b.

c.

3.

4.

5.

	Job 106	Job 107	Total

Problem 3-19

Name _____

1. _____

	a.		
a.			
b.			
c.			
d.			
e.			
f.			
g.			
h.			
i.			
j.			
k.			

(No. 1. — Continued)

l.								
m.								

2. Space for T-accounts has been provided on the following page.

3. _____

4.   CELESTIAL DISPLAYS , INC.

2.

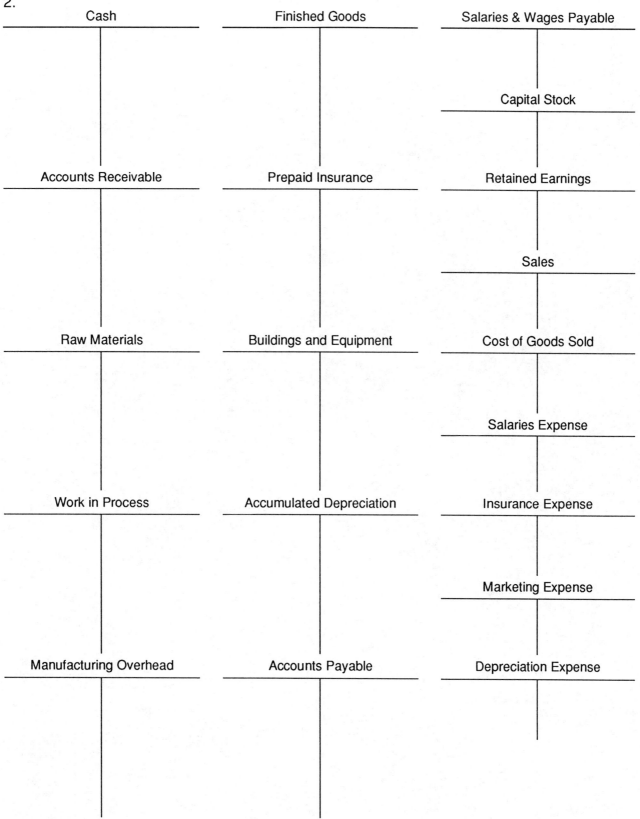

Cash	Finished Goods	Salaries & Wages Payable
Accounts Receivable	Prepaid Insurance	Capital Stock
		Retained Earnings
		Sales
Raw Materials	Buildings and Equipment	Cost of Goods Sold
		Salaries Expense
Work in Process	Accumulated Depreciation	Insurance Expense
		Marketing Expense
Manufacturing Overhead	Accounts Payable	Depreciation Expense

Problem 3-20   Name _____

1.

_____
_____
_____
_____
_____
_____
_____
_____
_____

2.

_____
_____
_____
_____

3.

		Departments		Total
		Res. & Docu.	Litigation	

4.

		Research & Documents	Litigation

Problem 3-21

Name _____

1.

2.

3.

4.

5.

6.

7.

8.

Problem 3-22

Name _____

1.

2.

3.

4.

5.

Problem 3-23   Name _____

1.

a.				
b.				
c.				
d.				
e.				
f.				
g.				
h.				
i.				
j.				

k.

l.

2.

| Accounts Receivable | Finished Goods | Sales |

| Raw Materials | Accumulated Depreciation | Cost of Goods Sold |

| | | Salaries Expense |

| | | Advertising Expense |

| Work in Process | Salaries & Wages Payable | Depreciation Expense |

| | | Rent Expense |

| Manufacturing Overhead | Accounts Payable | Miscellaneous Expense |

3. _____ SOUTHWORTH COMPANY _____

4.

5.　　　　　　　　　　　　SOUTHWORTH COMPANY

6.

Problem 3-24   Name _____

1.

| Cash | Finished Goods | Salaries & Wages Payable |

| Accounts Receivable | Prepaid Insurance | Capital Stock |

| | | Retained Earnings |

| | | Sales |

| Raw Materials | Plant & Equipment | Cost of Goods Sold |

| | | Salaries Expense |

| Work in Process | Accumulated Depreciation | Insurance Expense |

| | | Advertising Expense |

| Manufacturing Overhead | Accounts Payable | Depreciation Expense |

| | | Miscellaneous Expense |

2. _____   TOP-PRODUCTS, INC. _____

3.

4. TOP-PRODUCTS, INC.

5.

Name _____

1. a. _____

b. _____

2. a.

	Cutting Department	Machining Department	Assembly Department	

b.

3.

4. a.

b.

	Cutting Department			Machining Department			Assembly Department			Total Plant		

Problem 4-14

Name _____

1.

	Quantity Schedule	Equivalent Units		
		Materials	Labor	Overhead

2.

	Costs	Equivalent Units (EU)		
		Materials	Labor	Overhead

Problem 4-15

Name _____

1., 2., and 3.
Quantity schedule and equivalent units

	Quantity Schedule	Equivalent Units	
		Materials	Conversion

Total and unit costs

	Total	Materials	Conversion	Whole Unit

Cost reconciliation

	Costs	Equivalent Units (EU)	
		Materials	Conversion

Problem 4-16

1., 2., and 3.
Quantity schedule and equivalent units

	Quantity Schedule	Equivalent Units	
		Materials	Conversion

Total and unit costs

	Total	Materials	Conversion	Whole Unit

Cost reconciliation

	Costs	Equivalent Units (EU)	
		Materials	Conversion

Problem 4-17   Name _____

1., 2., and 3.

Quantity schedule and equivalent units

| | Quantity Schedule | Equivalent Units | |
		Materials	Conversion

Total and unit costs

	Total	Materials	Conversion	Whole Unit

Cost reconciliation

| | Costs | Equivalent Units (EU) | |
		Materials	Conversion

Problem 4-18

1., 2., and 3.

Quantity schedule and equivalent units

	Quantity Schedule	Equivalent Units	
		Materials	Conversion

Total and unit costs

	Total	Materials	Conversion	Whole Unit

Cost reconciliation

	Costs	Equivalent Units (EU)	
		Materials	Conversion

Problem 4-19

Name _____

1.

Quantity schedule and equivalent units

	Quantity Schedule	Equivalent Units	
		Materials	Labor & OVH.

Total and unit costs

	Total	Materials	Labor & OVH.	Whole Unit

Cost reconciliation

	Costs	Equivalent Units (EU)	
		Materials	Labor & OVH.

2. _____

_____

_____

_____

_____

_____

_____

_____

_____

_____

_____

_____

_____

_____

_____

_____

Problem 4-20

Name _____

Quantity schedule and equivalent units

	Quantity Schedule	Equivalent Units	
		Materials	Conversion

Total and unit costs

	Total	Materials	Conversion	Whole Unit

Cost reconciliation

	Costs	Equivalent Units (EU)	
		Materials	Conversion

Problem 4-21   Name _____

1.

2.

	Quantity Schedule	Equivalent Units	
		Materials	Conversion

3.

	Total Cost	Materials	Conversion	Whole Unit

4.

5. _____

_____

_____

_____

_____

_____

_____

_____

Problem 4-22   Name _____

1.

a.			
b.			
c.			
d.			
e.			
f.			
g.			

2.

Work in Process—Bottling	Work in Process—Blending

Manufacturing Overhead	Finished Goods

Raw Materials	Accounts Payable

Salaries & Wages Payable	Sales

Accounts Receivable	Cost of Goods Sold

Name _____

3.

Quantity schedule and equivalent units

	Quantity Schedule	Equivalent Units		
		Materials	Labor	Overhead

Total and unit costs

	Total Cost	Materials	Labor	Overhead	Whole Unit

Cost reconciliation

	Total Cost	Equivalent Units (above)		
		Materials	Labor	Overhead

Problem 4-23

Name _____

1.

	Materials	Conversion

	Total Cost	Materials	Conversion	Whole Unit

2.

	Work in Process	Finished Goods	Total

3.

	Work in Process	Finished Goods	Total

	Debit	Credit

4.

Problem 4-24   Name _____

1. _____

a.

b.

c.

d.

e.

f.

g.

2.

Work in Process—Assembly	Work in Process—Testing and Packaging

Manufacturing Overhead	Finished Goods

Raw Materials	Accounts Payable

Salaries & Wages Payable	Sales

Accounts Receivable	Cost of Goods Sold

3.

Quantity schedule and equivalent units

	Quantity Schedule	Equivalent Units		
		Materials	Labor	Overhead

Total and unit costs

	Total Cost	Materials	Labor	Overhead	Whole Unit

Cost reconciliation

	Total Cost	Equivalent Units (above)		
		Materials	Labor	Overhead

1., 2., and 3.

Activity	Activity Classification	Examples of Traceable Costs	Examples of Cost Drivers

Problem 5-10 (Continued)

1., 2., and 3.

Name _____

Activity	Activity Classification	Examples of Traceable Costs	Examples of Cost Drivers

Problem 5-11

Name _____

1. _____

		Deluxe	Regular

2.

Activity Center	(a) Estimated Overhead Cost	(b) Expected Activity	(a) ÷ (b) Predetermined Overhead Rate

3. a.

	Deluxe Model		Regular Model	
	Expected Activity	Amount	Expected Activity	Amount

3.b.

		Deluxe	Regular

4.

Problem 5-12

1.   YEDDER ENTERPRISES

	19X6		19X5	
	Amount	Percent*	Amount	Percent*

*As a percentage of total sales in each year.

2.

3. _____

_____

_____

_____

_____

_____

_____

_____

_____

_____

_____

_____

_____

_____

_____

_____

_____

_____

_____

_____

_____

_____

_____

_____

_____

_____

_____

_____

_____

_____

_____

_____

_____

_____

_____

_____

_____

_____

_____

_____

_____

_____

_____

_____

_____

Problem 5-13   Name _____

1. _____

		Mono-circuit	Bi-circuit

2.

Activity Center	(a) Estimated Overhead Cost	(b) Expected Activity	(a) ÷ (b) Predetermined Overhead Rate

3. a.

	Mono-circuit		Bi-circuit	
	Expected Activity	Amount	Expected Activity	Amount

107

3. b.

	Mono-circuit						Bi-circuit						

4.

1.   LEE ENTERPRISES

	19X6		19X5	
	Amount	Percent*	Amount	Percent*

*As a percentage of total sales in each year.

2.

3.

Problem 5-15

Name _____

1.

Activity Center	(a) Estimated Overhead Costs	(b) Expected Activity	(a) ÷ (b) Predetermined Overhead Rate

2. a.

b.

Work in Process

DM
DL
MO

Labor Related
Activity Center

Production Orders
Activity Center

Manufacturing Overhead

Product Testing
Activity Center

Template Etching
Activity Center

General Factory
Activity Center

Problem 5-15 (No. 3. – Continued)

3. a.

Activity Center	(a) Predetermined Overhead Rate	(b) Actual Activity	(a) x (b) Applied Overhead Cost

b.

4.

	Activity Center			
	Labor Related	Purchase Orders	Product Testing	Template Etching	General Factory
Total				

Name _____

1.

	Product				Total
	A	B	C	D	

2.

Problem 5-17

Name _____

1.

Activity Center	(a) Estimated Overhead Costs	(b) Expected Activity	(a) ÷ (b) Predetermined Overhead Rate

2. a.

b.

Work in Process

DM
DL
MO

Manufacturing Overhead

Labor Related
Activity Center

Production Orders
Activity Center

Material Handling
Activity Center

Testing
Activity Center

General Factory
Activity Center

117

Problem 5-17 (Continued)

3. a.

Activity Center	(a) Predetermined Overhead Rate	(b) Actual Activity	(a) x (b) Applied Overhead Cost

b.

4.

		Activity Center			
	Labor Related	Production Orders	Material Handling	Testing	General Factory
Total					

Problem 5-18   Name _____

1.

	Product				Total
	A	B	C	D	

2.

Name _____

1.

Activity Center	(1) Estimated Overhead Cost	(2) Expected Activity	(1) ÷ (2) Predetermined Overhead Rate

2. a.

b.

c.

d.

e.

f.

g.

h.

i. Computation of manufacturing overhead cost applied to production:

Activity Center	(1) Predetermined Overhead Rate	(2) Actual Activity	(1) x (2) Applied Overhead Cost

j.

k.

3. See the T-accounts on pages 124-25.

Problem 5-19 (Continued)

Name _____

4.

Total	Machining	Purchase Orders	Parts Management	Testing	General Factory

5. _____   JARVIS COMPANY

Accounts Receivable

Finished Goods

Sales

Cost of Goods Sold

Raw Materials

Accumulated Depreciation

Commissions Expense

Administrative Salary Expense

Work in Process

Accounts Payable

Sales Travel Expense

Advertising Expense

Problem 5-19 (No. 5. – Continued)   Name _____

| Manufacturing Overhead | Salaries and Wages Payable | Depreciation Expense |

Machining Activity Center

Testing Activity Center

Purchase Order Activity Center

General Factory Activity Center

Parts Management
Activity Center

1.

	12/31/97		12/31/98	
	Amount	Percentage*	Amount	Percentage*

*Percentage figures may not add down due to rounding.

1. (Continued)

2.

3.

Name _____

1. _____
_____
_____
_____
_____
_____
_____
_____

2. _____
_____
_____
_____
_____
_____
_____
_____
_____
_____
_____
_____
_____
_____
_____
_____
_____
_____
_____
_____
_____
_____
_____
_____
_____
_____
_____
_____
_____
_____
_____
_____
_____

3.   FRANKEL COMPANY

Problem 6-12

Name _____

1. _____

_____

_____

_____

_____

_____

_____

_____

_____

_____

_____

2. _____

_____

_____

_____

_____

_____

_____

_____

_____

_____

_____

_____

_____

_____

_____

_____

3. _____

_____

_____

_____

_____

_____

_____

_____

_____

4. _____

_____

_____

Problem 6-13   Name _____

1.

	Year	Number of Leagues (X)	Total Cost (Y)	XY	X²	

2. _____

3. _____

_____

_____

_____

_____

_____

_____

_____

_____

_____

_____

_____

4.

1.   THE HOUSE OF ORGANS, INC.

2. _____   THE HOUSE OF ORGANS, INC. _____

	Total	Per Unit

3.

1.

	Level of Activity			
	60,000 MH		80,000 MH	

2.

	Maintenance Cost		Machine-Hours	

3.

Problem 6-16   Name _____

1. a. _____
   b. _____
   c. _____
   d. _____
   e. _____
   f. _____
   g. _____
   h. _____
   i. _____

2. _____
   _____
   _____
   _____
   _____
   _____
   _____
   _____
   _____
   _____
   _____
   _____
   _____
   _____
   _____
   _____
   _____
   _____
   _____
   _____
   _____
   _____
   _____
   _____
   _____
   _____
   _____
   _____
   _____
   _____
   _____
   _____
   _____
   _____

Name _____

1.

Name _____

2. _____

Problem 6-18   Name _____

1.

Month	Meals Served (000)(X)	Total Cost (Y)	XY	X^2

2.

Name _____

1.

	Number of Ingots	Power Cost

2. (Place your scattergraph on the following page; use the space below for supporting computations.)

Problem 6-20   Name _____

1.

Month	Number of Ingots (X)	Power Cost (Y)	XY	X²

2. _____

_____

_____

_____

_____

_____

_____

_____

_____

_____

_____

_____

_____

_____

_____

_____

_____

_____

_____

_____

_____

_____

_____

_____

1.

2.

3.

Problem 6-22

Name _____

1.

Quarter	Units Sold (X)(000)	Shipping Expense (Y)	XY	X^2

2. _____ ALDEN COMPANY _____

Name _____

1. _____
   _____
   _____
   _____
   _____
   _____

2. _____
   _____

3. _____
   _____
   _____

4. a. _____
   _____
   _____
   _____
   _____

   b. _____

5. _____

	Last Year: 28,000 units		Proposed: 42,000 units*	
	Total	Per Unit	Total	Per Unit

   _____
   _____
   _____
   _____
   _____
   _____

6. _____
   _____
   _____
   _____
   _____
   _____
   _____

Name _____

1. _____
_____
_____
_____
_____
_____
_____
_____
_____

2. Graph paper for preparing the CVP graph has been provided on the following page.

3. _____
_____
_____
_____
_____
_____
_____
_____
_____
_____
_____

4. _____
_____
_____
_____
_____
_____
_____
_____
_____
_____

5. _____
_____
_____
_____
_____
_____
_____
_____
_____
_____
_____

2.

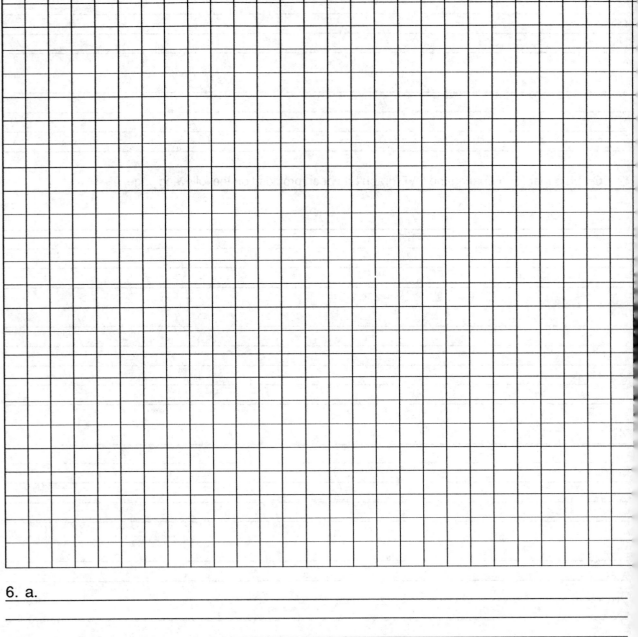

6. a. _____

_____

_____

_____

_____

_____

_____

b. _____

_____

_____

_____

_____

_____

Name _____

1. _____

	Total	Per Unit	Percentage

2. _____

3. _____

4. _____

5. a.

	Per Unit	Percentage

b.

	Not Automated			Automated		
	Total	Per Unit	%	Total	Per Unit	%

c.

Problem 7-13

Name _____

1.

	Product			Total
	A	B	C	

2.

3.

Problem 7-14

Name _____

1. _____

_____

_____

_____

_____

_____

_____

_____

_____

_____

_____

_____

_____

_____

_____

_____

_____

_____

_____

2. _____

_____

_____

_____

_____

_____

_____

_____

_____

_____

_____

_____

_____

_____

_____

_____

_____

_____

_____

_____

_____

_____

_____

_____

_____

Problem 7-15

1. a.

Alvaro		Bazan		Total	
Amount	Percent	Amount	Percent	Amount	Percent

b. Space has been provided on the following page.

2. a.

Alvaro		Bazan		Cano		Total	
Amount	Percent	Amount	Percent	Amount	Percent	Amount	Percent

163

1. b.

2. b.

3.

Name _____

1. (1) _____
   (2) _____
   _____
   (3) _____
   (4) _____
   (5) _____
   (6) _____
   (7) _____
   (8) _____
   (9) _____
   (10) _____

2. a. _____
   _____
   _____

   b. _____
   _____
   _____

   c. _____
   _____
   _____

   d. _____
   _____
   _____

   e. _____
   _____
   _____

   f. _____
   _____
   _____

   g. _____
   _____
   _____

   h. _____
   _____
   _____
   _____
   _____

Problem 7-17

Name _____

1. _____

_____

_____

_____

_____

_____

_____

_____

_____

_____

_____

_____

_____

2. Graph paper has been provided on the following page.

3. _____

_____

_____

_____

_____

_____

_____

_____

4. _____

_____

_____

_____

_____

_____

_____

5. _____

_____

_____

_____

_____

_____

_____

_____

2.

Name _____

1. a. _____

b. _____

2. _____

3.

4.

5.

6. a.

b.

c.

1. April's Income Statement:

	Standard		Deluxe		Pro		Total	
	Amount	Percent	Amount	Percent	Amount	Percent	Amount	Percent

Problem 7-19 (No. 1 Continued)

Name _____

May's Income Statement:

	Standard		Deluxe		Pro		Total	
	Amount	Percent	Amount	Percent	Amount	Percent	Amount	Percent

2.

3.

4.

.

Problem 7-20

Name _____

1.

	Unit Sales Price	Unit Variable Expense	Unit Contribution Margin	Volume (Units)	Total Contribution Margin	Fixed Expenses	Net Income

2.

4.

Name _____

1. _____

2.

3.

Name _____

1.

	Present			Proposed		
	Amount	Per Unit	Percent	Amount	Per Unit	Percent

2.

	Present	Proposed
a.		
b.		
c.		

3. _____

4. _____

Problem 7-23

Name _____

1. a. _____

PUTREX COMPANY

	Total	Per Unit	Percent

Problem 7-23 (Continued)

Name _____

1. b.

c.

d.

2. a.

PUTREX COMPANY

	Total	Per Unit	Percent

b.

3. _____

Problem 8-8

Name _____

1. _____

	Year 1	Year 2

2. _____

	Year 1	Year 2

Name _____

1. a.

b.

2. a.

b.

Name _____

3. _____

Problem 8-10

Name _____

	Absorption Costing	Variable Costing
1. a. and b.		
2. Absorption costing income statement:		
3. Variable costing income statement:		

4.

5.

Problem 8-11

Name _____

1.

a.

b.

c.

2.

3.

a.

b.

c.

Problem 8-12   Name _____

1. a. and b.

	Absorption Costing	Variable Costing

2.

	May	June

3.

	May	June

4. _____

_____

_____

_____

_____

_____

_____

_____

_____

_____

_____

_____

_____

_____

_____

_____

_____

_____

_____

_____

_____

Name _____

	19x1	19x2	19x3
1.			

	19x1	19x2	19x3
2. a.			
b.			

3.

4.

5. a. _____

_____

_____

_____

_____

_____

_____

_____

_____

b. _____

_____

_____

_____

_____

_____

_____

_____

_____

_____

		19x1	19x2	19x3

Problem 9-9

1.

	July	August	September	October

2.

3.

	July	August	September	Third Quarter

1.

	Month			Quarter	
	April	May	June		

2.

	Month			Quarter	
	April	May	June		

3.

Name _____

1.

PHOTOTEC, INC.

2. _____   PHOTOTEC, INC. _____

3. _____   PHOTOTEC, INC. _____

Problem 9-12   Name _____

1.

	Order Size in Units				
	300	600	900	1,200	1,500

2.

Problem 9-13   Name _____

1. _____

_____

_____

_____

_____

_____

_____

_____

_____

_____

_____

_____

_____

_____

_____

_____

_____

_____

_____

_____

_____

2. _____

_____

_____

_____

_____

_____

_____

_____

_____

_____

_____

_____

_____

_____

_____

_____

_____

_____

_____

_____

_____

_____

Problem 9-14

Name _____

1. _____

2. _____

3. _____

Problem 9-15   Name _____

1. The sales budget for the third quarter:

	July	August	September	Quarter

2. The production budget for July through October:

	July	August	September	October

3. The materials purchases budget for the third quarter:

	July	August	September	Quarter

3. The schedule of expected cash payments:

	July	August	September	Quarter

Problem 9-16

1. a. Schedule of budgeted cash collections:

	19x2 Quarter				Total
	First	Second	Third	Fourth	

b. Schedule of budgeted cash payments for merchandise purchases:

	19x2 Quarter				Total
	First	Second	Third	Fourth	

Problem 9-16 (Continued)

2.

	19x2 Quarter				Year
	First	Second	Third	Fourth	

3. Cash budget for 19x2:

	19x2 Quarter				Year
	First	Second	Third	Fourth	

Problem 9-17

Name _____

	July	August	Sept.	Quarter
1. Collections on sales:				
2. a. Inventory purchases budget:				
b. Schedule of expected cash disbursements for inventory:				

3.   JANUS PRODUCTS

		July	August	Sept.	Quarter

Problem 9-18

Name _____

1. Schedule of expected cash collections:

	April	May	June	Quarter

2. a. Purchases budget:

	April	May	June	Quarter

b. Schedule of expected cash dispursements for purchases:

	April	May	June	Quarter

Problem 9-18 (Continued)　　　　　　Name _____

3. Schedule of expected cash disbursements — expenses:

	April	May	June	Quarter

4. Cash budget:

	April	May	June	Quarter

5.   NORDIC COMPANY

6.　　　　　　　　　　　　　　　　NORDIC COMPANY

Problem 9-19

Name _____

1. _____
_____
_____

2. _____
_____
_____
_____
_____
_____
_____
_____

3. _____
_____
_____
_____
_____
_____

4. _____
_____
_____
_____
_____
_____
_____
_____
_____
_____
_____

.a. _____
_____

b. _____
_____
_____
_____

Problem 9-20

Name _____

1.

	Order size			
	100	200	300	400

2.

3.

225

Problem 9-21   Name _____

1. Collection pattern: _____

_____
_____
_____
_____
_____
_____
_____
_____
_____
_____
_____
_____
_____

Schedule of expected cash collections:

2. _____   HOUSEHALL COMPANY, LTD.   _____

3.

Problem 9-22

1.

	April	May	June	Quarter

2. Material #208:

	April	May	June	Quarter

Material #311:

	April	May	June	Quarter

3. Direct labor budget:

	Units Produced	Direct Labor Hours		Cost Per DLH	Total Cost
		Per Unit	Total		

4. Manufacturing overhead budget:

Name _____

1. a.

_____   _____   _____
_____   _____   _____
_____   _____   _____
_____   _____   _____

b.

2. a.

_____   _____   _____
_____   _____   _____
_____   _____   _____
_____   _____   _____

_____
_____
_____

b. _____
_____
_____
_____

3. _____   _____   _____
_____   _____   _____
_____   _____   _____
_____   _____   _____

_____
_____
_____
_____
_____
_____
_____
_____

Name _____

1. _____

_____

_____

_____

_____

_____

_____

_____

2. a. _____

_____

_____

_____

_____　　　　_____　　　　_____

_____　　　　_____　　　　_____

_____　　　　_____　　　　_____

_____

_____

_____

_____

_____

_____

　b. _____

_____

_____

_____

_____

_____

_____

_____

_____

_____

_____

_____

_____

_____

_____

_____

_____

3. _____   _____   _____

Problem 10-13   Name _____

1. a. _____   _____   _____
   _____   _____   _____
   _____   _____   _____
   _____   _____   _____

b. _____   _____   _____
   _____   _____   _____
   _____   _____   _____
   _____   _____   _____

1. c.

_____   _____   _____
_____   _____   _____
_____   _____   _____
_____   _____   _____

2.

3. _____

Name _____

1. a.

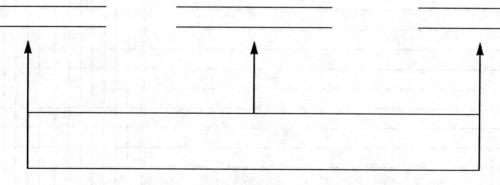

b.

2. a.

b.

3.

_____   _____   _____
_____   _____   _____
_____   _____   _____
_____   _____   _____

Name _____

5.

Problem 10-15   Name _____

1. a., b., and c.

	Month			
	1	2	3	4

2. _____

3. a. and b.

Name _____

1. a. _____

_____

_____

_____

_____

_____

_____

_____

_____

_____

_____

_____

_____

_____

_____

_____

_____

_____

_____

_____

_____

b. _____

_____

_____

_____

_____

_____   _____   _____

_____   _____   _____

_____   _____   _____

_____   _____   _____

c. _____

_____

_____

2. a. _____

_____

_____

_____

_____

_____

_____

_____

_____

_____

_____

_____

_____

_____

b. _____

_____

_____

_____

_____

_____   _____   _____

_____   _____   _____

_____   _____   _____

_____   _____   _____

c. _____

_____

_____

_____

_____

_____

Problem 10-17

1.

2.

3.

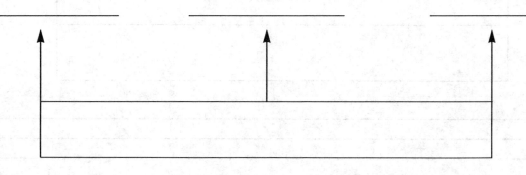

4.

5.

6. _____

_____   _____   _____
_____   _____   _____
_____   _____   _____
_____   _____   _____

7.

	Standard Quantity or Hours	Standard Price or Rate	Standard Cost

Problem 10-18   Name _____

1. _____
_____
_____
_____
_____
_____
_____
_____
_____
_____
_____
_____
_____
_____
_____
_____
_____
_____
_____
_____
_____
_____
_____

2. _____
_____
_____
_____
_____
_____
_____
_____
_____
_____
_____
_____
_____
_____
_____
_____
_____
_____
_____
_____
_____

3.

	Standard Quantity or Time per Batch	Standard Price or Rate per Quarter	Standard Cost

Problem 10-19

1. a., b., and c.

	Month			
	1	2	3	4

2. a.

2. b. _____

_____

_____

_____

_____

_____

_____

_____

_____

_____

c. _____

_____

_____

_____

_____

_____

_____

_____

_____

_____

_____

_____

_____

_____

3. a. and b. _____

_____

_____

_____

_____

_____

_____

_____

_____

_____

_____

_____

Name _____

1.

_____   _____   _____
_____   _____   _____
_____   _____   _____
_____   _____   _____

2. _____　　_____　　_____

_____　　_____　　_____

_____　　_____　　_____

_____　　_____　　_____

3.

Problem 10-20 (Continued)   Name _____

4. a. and b.

| | Month | | |
	April	May	June

5.

Problem 10-21   Name _____

1. _____
_____
_____
_____
_____
_____
_____

2. a. and b.

| | Lot Number | | | Total |
	30	31	32	

3. _____
_____
_____
_____
_____

4. a. and b.

| | Lot Number | | | Total |
	30	31	32	

5. _____

_____

_____

_____

_____

_____

_____

_____

_____

_____

_____

_____

_____

_____

_____

_____

_____

_____

_____

_____

_____

_____

_____

_____

Problem 10-22

Name _____

1. a.

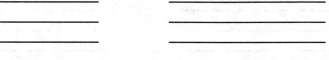

b.

2. a.

_____   _____   _____
_____   _____   _____
_____   _____   _____
_____   _____   _____

b.

3. a. _____   _____   _____
_____   _____   _____
_____   _____   _____
_____   _____   _____

_____
_____
_____
_____
_____
_____
_____
_____
_____

b. _____
_____
_____
_____
_____
_____

4. _____
_____
_____
_____
_____
_____
_____
_____
_____
_____
_____
_____
_____
_____
_____
_____
_____
_____
_____

Problem 10-23   Name _____

1. _____

2. a. _____

_____

_____

   b. _____

_____

_____

_____

_____

_____

_____

_____

_____

_____

_____

_____

_____

_____

_____

_____

_____

_____

_____

_____

_____

_____

_____

_____

_____

_____

_____

_____

_____

_____

_____

_____

_____

_____

_____

_____

1.

3. _____   _____   _____

_____   _____   _____

_____   _____   _____

_____   _____   _____

Problem 11-10

1.

2.

3. Variable manufacturing overhead variances:

_____

Fixed manufacturing overhead variances:

_____   _____   _____

4. _____

Problem 11-11   Name _____

1. _____
_____
_____
_____
_____
_____
_____

2. _____
_____
_____
_____
_____
_____
_____
_____

3. a. Variable overhead spending and efficiency variances:

_____   _____   _____
_____   _____   _____
_____   _____   _____
_____   _____   _____

_____
_____
_____
_____
_____
_____
_____

b. Fixed overhead budget and volume variances:

_____   _____   _____
_____   _____   _____
_____   _____   _____
_____   _____   _____

Problem 11-11 (Continued)

Name _____

3. b. (Continued)

4.

Problem 11-12

Name _____

1. _____

_____

_____

_____

_____

_____

_____

_____

_____

_____

_____

_____

_____

_____

_____

2. _____

3. Variable overhead variances:

_____   _____   _____

_____   _____   _____

_____   _____   _____

_____   _____   _____

_____

_____

_____

_____

_____

_____

_____

_____

Fixed overhead variances:

_____   _____   _____

_____   _____   _____

_____   _____   _____

_____   _____   _____

Verification of variances:

4.

Problem 11-13   Name _____

1. _____
_____
_____
_____
_____
_____

2. _____
_____
_____
_____
_____

3.   SHIPLEY COMPANY
_____

Budgeted machine-hours
Actual machine-hours

Name _____

1. _____
_____
_____
_____
_____
_____
_____
_____

2. _____
_____
_____
_____
_____
_____

3. a. _____

   b.   Manufacturing Overhead

4. Variable overhead variances:

_____   _____   _____
_____   _____   _____
_____   _____   _____
_____   _____   _____

_____
_____
_____
_____
_____
_____
_____

Fixed overhead variances:

_____   _____   _____
_____   _____   _____
_____   _____   _____
_____   _____   _____

Summary of variances:

5.

Problem 11-15

Name _____

1.   THE ROWE COMPANY

Budgeted direct labor-hours

	Cost Formula	Direct Labor Hours		
		40,000	50,000	60,000

2.

3. a.

Manufacturing Overhead

Problem 11-15 (Continued) Name ____________________

b. Variable overhead variances:

Fixed overhead variances:

Problem 11-16

Name _____

1. and 2.

		Per Direct Labor Hour		
		Variable	Fixed	Total

3.

Denominator Activity: 40,000 DLH		Denominator Activity: 50,000 DLH	

4. a.

_____

_____

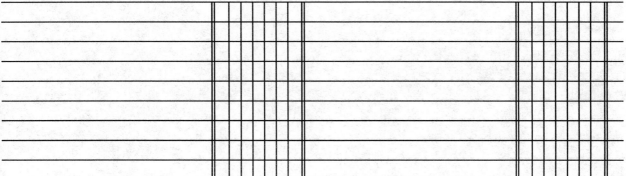

Manufacturing Overhead

c. Variable overhead variances:

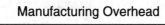

283

Fixed overhead variances:

_____　　　_____　　　_____
_____　　　_____　　　_____
_____　　　_____　　　_____
_____　　　_____　　　_____

Summary of variances:

5.

1. _____

_____

_____

_____

_____

_____

_____

_____

_____

_____

_____

_____

_____

_____

_____

_____

2.

3. Graph paper has been provided on the following page.

4. a. Fixed overhead variances:

3.

_____
_____
_____
_____
_____
_____
_____
_____
_____
_____
_____
_____
_____
_____
_____
_____
_____
_____
_____
_____
_____

b. See graph paper provided.

. a. _____

b. See graph paper provided.

287

Problem 11-17 (Continued)   Name _____

4. b. and 5. b.

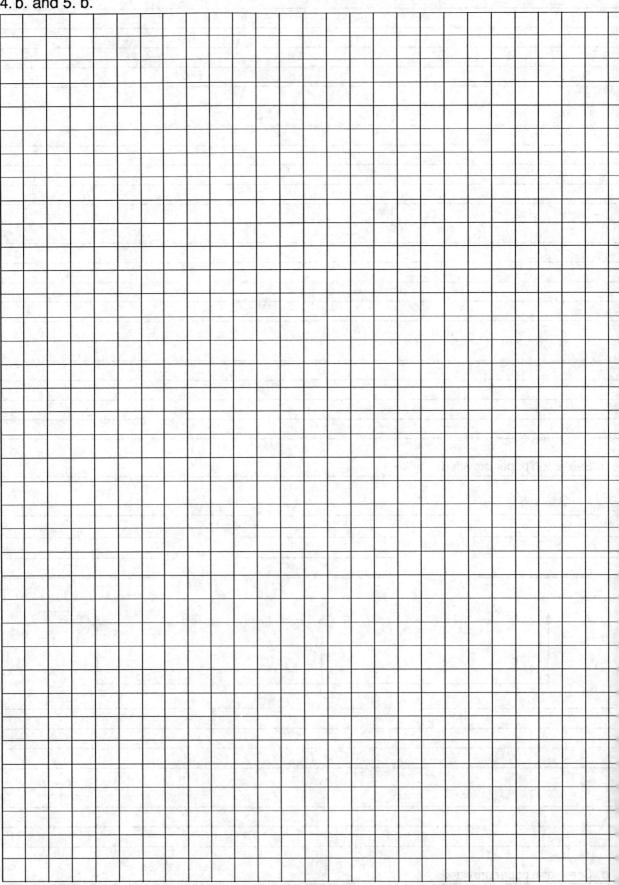

Name

Budgeted machine-hours

Actual machine-hours

Standard machine-hours allowed

Name _____

1.   THE DURRANT COMPANY

2.   THE DURRANT COMPANY

Budgeted machine-hours

Actual machine-hours

3.

4.

Name _____

1. _____

MASON COMPANY

2. _____

Budgeted machine-hours _____
Actual machine-hours _____
Standard machine-hours _____

Overhead Costs	Cost Formula (per MH)	Actual Costs Incurred (1)	Budget Based on ___ Hrs. (2)	Budget Based on ___ Hrs. (3)	Total Variance (1) - (3)	Spending Variance (1) - (2)	Efficiency Variance (2) - (3)

Problem 11-21   Name _____

1. _____   ELGIN COMPANY   _____
_____
_____

	Cost Formula	Percentage of Capacity		
		80%	90%	100%

2. _____
_____
_____
_____
_____

Name _____

3. ELGIN COMPANY

Budgeted machine-hours

Standard machine-hours

Actual machine-hours

4.

4. _____

_____

_____

_____

_____

_____

_____

_____

_____

_____

_____

_____

_____

_____

_____

_____

_____

_____

_____

_____

_____

_____

_____

5. _____

_____

_____

_____

_____

_____

_____

_____

_____

_____

_____

_____

_____

_____

_____

_____

_____

_____

_____

Name _____

1.

Sales Territory

Total Company | Central | Eastern

Product Line

Central Territory | Awls | Pows

299

2. _____

3. _____

Problem 12-15   Name _____

1. _____

_____
_____
_____
_____
_____
_____
_____
_____
_____
_____
_____
_____
_____

2. _____

_____
_____
_____
_____
_____
_____
_____
_____
_____
_____

3.   See the statement on following page.

4. _____

_____
_____
_____
_____
_____
_____
_____
_____
_____
_____
_____
_____
_____
_____
_____
_____

3.

	Total		Southern Europe		Middle Europe		Northern Europe	
	Amount	Percent	Amount	Percent	Amount	Percent	Amount	Percent

Problem 12-16

Name _____

1.

Total Company		Wheat Cereal		Pancake Mix		Flour	

303

2. a. _____

b. _____

3. _____

Problem 12-17

Name _____

1.

2.

	Company		
	A	B	C

2. _____

Problem 12-18

Name _____

1. _____

	Present	New Line	Total

2. _____

3. _____

4. a. _____

	Present	New Line	Total

b. _____

Problem 12-19

1.

	Beginning Balances	Ending Balances	

2.

Name _____

1. _____
_____
_____
_____
_____
_____
_____
_____
_____
_____
_____
_____
_____

2. _____
_____
_____
_____
_____
_____

3. _____
_____
_____
_____
_____
_____
_____
_____
_____
_____
_____
_____
_____
_____
_____

4. _____
_____

5. _____

6. _____

7. _____
_____
_____
_____
_____
_____

8. _____
_____
_____
_____
_____
_____
_____
_____
_____
_____
_____
_____
_____
_____
_____
_____
_____
_____
_____
_____
_____
_____
_____
_____
_____
_____
_____
_____
_____
_____
_____
_____
_____
_____

Name _____

1. _____

_____

_____

_____

_____

_____

2. a. _____

_____

_____

_____

_____

_____

_____

_____

_____

_____

_____

_____

_____

_____

b. _____

_____

_____

_____

_____

_____

_____

_____

_____

_____

_____

_____

_____

_____

_____

_____

_____

_____

3. a. _____

_____

_____

_____

_____

_____

_____

_____

_____

_____

_____

_____

_____

_____

b. _____

_____

_____

_____

_____

_____

_____

_____

_____

_____

_____

_____

_____

4. _____

_____

_____

_____

_____

_____

_____

_____

_____

_____

_____

_____

Name _____

Problem 12-22

1. Segments defined as product lines:

	Leather Division	Product Line		
		Garments	Shoes	Handbags

2. Segments defined as markets for the handbag product line:

	Handbags	Sales Market	
		Domestic	Foreign

3. _____

_____

_____

_____

_____

_____

_____

_____

_____

_____

_____

_____

_____

_____

_____

_____

_____

_____

_____

_____

_____

_____

_____

_____

_____

_____

_____

Problem 12-23

1. _____

2. _____

3. _____

5.

6.

7.

Problem 12-24

Name _____

1.

	Total Company		District A		District B		District C	
	Amount	Percent	Amount	Percent	Amount	Percent	Amount	Percent

2. _____

3. _____

Name _____

4. _____

Name _____

1.a.

b.

2.

3.

Name _____

1. a. _____
_____
_____
_____
_____
_____
_____

b. _____
_____
_____
_____
_____
_____
_____
_____

c. _____
_____
_____
_____
_____
_____

d. _____
_____
_____
_____
_____
_____

e. _____
_____
_____
_____
_____
_____

2. a. _____

_____

_____

_____

_____

_____

_____

_____

_____

_____

_____

_____

_____

_____

_____

_____

_____

_____

_____

_____

b. - e. _____

_____

_____

_____

_____

_____

_____

_____

_____

_____

_____

_____

_____

_____

_____

_____

_____

_____

_____

_____

Problem 12-27

Name _____

1.a.

_____

_____

_____

_____

b.

_____

_____

_____

_____

2. a. and b.

	Sales Volume		

3.

	Present Sales	New Sales	Total Sales	

Problem 12-28   Name _____

1. _____

_____

_____

_____

_____

_____

_____

_____

_____

_____

_____

_____

_____

_____

_____

_____

_____

_____

_____

_____

_____

_____

_____

2. _____

_____

_____

_____

_____

_____

_____

_____

_____

_____

_____

_____

_____

_____

_____

_____

_____

_____

_____

_____

_____

_____

_____

_____

Problem 12-29   Name _____

1. _____

_____
_____
_____
_____
_____
_____
_____
_____
_____
_____
_____
_____
_____
_____
_____
_____
_____
_____
_____
_____
_____
_____
_____

. _____
_____
_____
_____
_____
_____
_____
_____
_____
_____
_____
_____
_____
_____
_____
_____
_____
_____
_____

3. _____

_____
_____
_____
_____
_____
_____
_____
_____
_____
_____
_____
_____
_____
_____
_____
_____
_____
_____
_____
_____
_____
_____
_____
_____

4. _____

_____
_____
_____
_____
_____
_____
_____
_____
_____
_____
_____
_____
_____

1.

	Total		Line A		Line B		Line C	
	Amount	Percent	Amount	Percent	Amount	Percent	Amount	Percent

2.

3.

Problem 12-30 (Continued)

4. a.

	Total		Home Market		Foreign Market	
	Amount	Percent	Amount	Percent	Amount	Percent

4. b.

Problem 12-31   Name _____

1. _____

_____

_____

_____

_____

_____

_____

_____

_____

_____

_____

_____

_____

_____

_____

_____

_____

_____

_____

_____

_____

_____

_____

_____

_____

_____

_____

_____

_____

_____

_____

_____

_____

_____

_____

_____

_____

_____

_____

_____

_____

_____

_____

_____

_____

_____

_____

_____

Name _____

2. _____

Problem 13-11

Name _____

1. a. and b.

	5-Year Summary		
	Keep Old Press	Difference	Buy New Press

2.

Name _____

1. _____

Cost

Reason

Alternative Solution:

	Keep the Tour	Drop the Tour	Difference: Net Income Increase or (Decrease)

2. _____

Problem 13-13

Name _____

1.

2.

3.

4.

5.

6.

Name

Problem 13-14

1. _____

_____

_____

_____

_____

_____

_____

_____

	Differential Costs Per Unit		Total Differential Costs—40,000 Units	
	Make	Buy	Make	Buy

_____

_____

_____

2. a. _____

_____

_____

_____

	Differential Costs Per Unit		Total Differential Costs—50,000 Units	
	Make	Buy	Make	Buy

Problem 13-14 (Continued)   Name _____

2. b.

	Differential Costs Per Unit		Total Differential Costs—60,000 Units	
	Make	Buy	Make	Buy

3.

1. _____

_____

_____

_____

_____

_____

_____

_____

_____

_____

_____

_____

_____

_____

_____

_____

_____

_____

_____

_____

_____

_____

_____

_____

_____

_____

_____

_____

_____

_____

_____

_____

_____

_____

_____

_____

_____

_____

_____

_____

_____

_____

_____

_____

_____

_____

_____

2.

3.

Problem 13-16

Name _____

1. _____

	Plant Kept Open	Plant Closed	Difference: Net Income Increase or (Decrease)

Alternative Solution:

	Plant Kept Open	Plant Closed	Difference: Net Income Increase or (Decrease)

2. _____

Varification:

Problem 13-17

Name _____

1.

2.

3.

4.

5.

Problem 13-18   Name _____

1.

2.

3.

Name _____

1. Alternative Solution:

	Downtown Store Keep Open	Downtown Store Closed	Difference— Net Income Increase or (Decrease)

Problem 13-19

Name _____

1.

2.

	Variable	Fixed

Problem 13-20   Name _____

1. _____

2. _____

Problem 13-21   Name _____

1.

2.

Name _____

Item	Year(s)	Amount of Cash Flows	14% Factor	Present Value of Cash Flows

Problem 14-13

Name _____

1.

Item	Year(s)	Amount of Cash Flows	16% Factor	Present Value of Cash Flows

Problem 14-14

Name _____

1.

2.

Item	Year(s)	Amount of Cash Flows	12% Factor	Present Value of Cash Flows

Problem 14-15

1.

2.

Item	Year(s)	Amount of Cash Flows	18% Factor	Present Value of Cash Flows

Problem 14-16

1.

2.

3.

1.

Item	Year(s)	Amount of Cash Flows	16% Factor	Present Value of Cash Flows

2. _____

3. _____

Problem 14-18

Name _____

1. The total-cost approach:

Item	Year(s)	Amount of Cash Flows	16% Factor	Present Value of Cash Flows

2. The incremental-cost approach:

Item	Year(s)	Amount of Cash Flows	16% Factor	Present Value of Cash Flows

Problem 14-19   Name _____

1. _____

2. _____

3. a. _____

3. b.

4. a.

Problem 14-19 (No. 4. — continued)   Name _____

4. b. _____

Item	Year(s)	Amount of Cash Flow	Factor	Present Value of Cash Flows

Problem 14-20

1.

2.

Problem 14-21

Name _____

1.

Item	Year(s)	Amount of Cash Flows	18% Factor	Present Value of Cash Flows

Name _____

1.

2.

3.

4.

Problem 14-23

Name _____

1. a.

b.

c.

2. a.

b. _____

3. _____

Name _____

1.

2.

	Year(s)	Amount of Cash Flows	20% Factor	Present Value of Cash Flows

3.

	Year(s)	Amount of Cash Flows	20% Factor	Present Value of Cash Flows

4. a. _____

b.

Problem 14-25

Name _____

1.

	Year			
	1	2	3	4-12

2.

Item	Year(s)	Amount of Cash Flows	20% Factor	Present Value of Cash Flows

Problem 14-26   Name _____

1.

2.

3.

4.

1.

Item	Year(s)	Amount of Cash Flows	14% Factor	Present Value of Cash Flows

Name _____

1.

Items & Computations	Year(s)	(1) Amount	(2) Tax Effect	(1) x (2) After-Tax Cash Flows	10% Factor	Present Value of Cash Flows

2.

Items & Computations	Year(s)	(1) Amount	(2) Tax Effect	(1) x (2) After-Tax Cash Flows	12% Factor	Present Value of Cash Flows

1.

Items & Computations	Year(s)	(1) Amount	(2) Tax Effect	(1) x (2) After-Tax Cash Flows	14% Factor	Present Value of Cash Flows

Problem 13-16 (Continued)

Problem 13-16 (Continued)

2.

Items & Computations	Year(s)	(1) Amount	(2) Tax Effect	(1) x (2) After-Tax Cash Flows	14% Factor	Present Value of Cash Flows

Problem 15-11   Name _____

1. _____
_____
_____
_____
_____
_____
_____
_____
_____
_____
_____
_____

2. a., b., and c.

	Net Present Value	Profitability Index	Internal Rate of Return
First preference			
Second preference			
Third preference			
Fourth preference			
Fifth preference			

3. _____
_____
_____
_____
_____
_____
_____
_____
_____
_____
_____
_____
_____
_____
_____
_____
_____
_____
_____
_____
_____
_____

Name

1.

2.

Items & Computations	Year(s)	(1) Amount	(2) Tax Effect	(1) x (2) After-Tax Cash Flows	10% Factor	Present Value of Cash Flows

Name _____

1.

	Year				Total 1-10
	1	2	3	4-10	

Problem 15-13 (No. 2. — continued)

Name _____

Items & Computations	Year(s)	(1) Amount	(2) Tax Effect	(1) x (2) After-Tax Cash Flows	16% Factor	Present Value of Cash Flows

1.

Items & Computations	Year(s)	(1) Amount	(2) Tax Effect	(1) x (2) After-Tax Cash Flows	12% Factor	Present Value of Cash Flows

Problem 15-14 (No. 1. — continued)

Name _____

Items & Computations	Year(s)	(1) Amount	(2) Tax Effect	(1) x (2) After-Tax Cash Flows	12% Factor	Present Value of Cash Flows

2.

	Camera #1	Camera #2

Problem 15-15   Name _____

1. _____
_____
_____
_____
_____
_____
_____
_____
_____
_____
_____
_____

2. a., b., and c.

	Net Present Value	Profitability Index	Internal Rate of Return
First preference			
Second preference			
Third preference			
Fourth preference			
Fifth preference			

1.

Items & Computations	Year(s)	(1) Amount	(2) Tax Effect	(1) x (2) After-Tax Cash Flows	14% Factor	Present Value of Cash Flows

Problem 15-16 (Continued)

2.

Items & Computations	Year(s)	(1) Amount	(2) Tax Effect	(1) x (2) After-Tax Cash Flows	14% Factor	Present Value of Cash Flows

3.

Name _____

1.

2.

Items & Computations	Year(s)	(1) Amount	(2) Tax Effect	(1) x (2) After-Tax Cash Flows	10% Factor	Present Value of Cash Flows

Problem 13-18

1.

Items & Computations	Year(s)	(1) Amount	(2) Tax Effect	(1) x (2) After-Tax Cash Flows	12% Factor	Present Value of Cash Flows

Problem 15-18 (Continued)

Name _____

2.

Items & Computations	Year(s)	(1) Amount	(2) Tax Effect	(1) x (2) After-Tax Cash Flows	12% Factor	Present Value of Cash Flows

Name _____

Alternative 1:

Items & Computations	Year(s)	(1) Amount	(2) Tax Effect	(1) x (2) After-Tax Cash Flows	8% Factor	Present Value of Cash Flows

Problem 15-19

Name _____

Alternative 2:

Items & Computations	Year(s)	(1) Amount	(2) Tax Effect	(1) x (2) After-Tax Cash Flows	8% Factor	Present Value of Cash Flows

Name _____

1. _____

2. _____

3. _____

	Factory Admin.	Custodial Serv.	Personnel	Maintenance	Stamping	Assembly
1. Step method:						
2. Direct method:						

3.

4.

Problem 16-9

Name _____

1.

	Machine Tools Division	Special Products Division

2.

	Machine Tools Division	Special Products Division

3.

4.

5.

Food Services	Admin. Services	X-Ray Services	Outpatient Clinic	OB Care	General Hospital

Problem 16-10 (Continued)

Name _____

Food Services	Admin. Services	X-Ray Services	Outpatient Clinic	OB Care	General Hospital

Problem 16-10 (Continued)

Name _____

Computation of allocation rates:

1.

	Milling Department	Finishing Department	Total

2. a.

	Milling Department	Finishing Department	Total

b.

	Variable Costs	Fixed Costs	Total

	Grounds & Maint.	General Admin.	Laundry	Convention Center	Food Services	Lodging

Name _____

Grounds & Maint.	General Admin.	Laundry	Convention Center	Food Services	Lodging

Problem 16-12 (Continued)

Name _____

Computation of allocation rates:

Problem 16-13

Name _____

1.

2.

	Lines of Print	Total Cost

3.

	Division			Total
	A	B	C	

Problem 16-14

Name _____

1. and 2.

	Medical Services	Maintenance	Producing A	Producing B

Problem 16-14 (No. 1. and 2. — Continued)   Name _____

Supporting computations:

_____

_____

_____

_____

_____

_____

_____

_____

_____

_____

_____

_____

_____

_____

_____

_____

_____

_____

_____

_____

_____

_____

3. _____

_____

_____

_____

_____

_____

_____

_____

_____

_____

_____

_____

_____

_____

_____

_____

_____

1. and 2.　　　　　　　　　　　FOXBORO COMPANY

3. _____

Worksheet

	(1) Change	(2) Source or use?	(3) Cash Flow Effect	(4) Adjust- ments	(5) Adjusted Effect	(6) Classi- fication

Problem 17-10

1.

2. _____   FOXBORO COMPANY   _____

3. _____

_____

_____

_____

_____

_____

_____

_____

_____

_____

_____

_____

_____

_____

_____

_____

_____

_____

_____

_____

_____

_____

_____

_____

_____

_____

_____

_____

_____

_____

_____

_____

_____

_____

_____

_____

_____

_____

_____

_____

_____

_____

_____

_____

_____

_____

_____

1. and 2.   EATON COMPANY

Problem 17-11 (Continued)

Name _____

Worksheet

	(1) Change	(2) Source or use?	(3) Cash Flow Effect	(4) Adjust- ments	(5) Adjusted Effect	(6) Classi- fication

Problem 17-12

Name _____

1.

2. _____ EATON COMPANY _____

Worksheet

Transaction	Operating	Investing	Financing	Source, Use, or Neither	Reported in Separate Schedule

Name _____

1. and 2. ALLIED PRODUCTS

3. _____

Worksheet

(1) Change	(2) Source or use?	(3) Cash Flow Effect	(4) Adjust- ments	(5) Adjusted Effect	(6) Classi- fication

Problem 17-15

Name _____

1.

2.   ALLIED PRODUCTS

Problem 17-16

Name _____

Supporting computations:

_____

_____

_____

Plant and Equipment	Accumulated Depreciation

_____

DAMOCLES COMPANY

Problem 17-16 (Continued)

Worksheet

	(1) Change	(2) Source or use?	(3) Cash Flow Effect	(4) Adjust- ments	(5) Adjusted Effect	(6) Classi- fication

Problem 17-17 (Continued)

Worksheet

	(1) Change	(2) Source or use?	(3) Cash Flow Effect	(4) Adjust- ments	(5) Adjusted Effect	(6) Classi- fication

2. _____ ALCORN PRODUCTS _____

3.

Name _____

Problem 17-19

Name _____

Supporting computations:

_____

_____

_____

Plant and Equipment	Accumulated Depreciation

LUANG CORPORATION

Worksheet

(1) Change		(2) Source or use?	(3) Cash Flow Effect	(4) Adjustments	(5) Adjusted Effect	(6) Classification

Problem 18-9

Name _____

1. a. – g.

	This Year	Last Year

2. a.　　　　　　　　　　MODERN BUILDING SUPPLY

	This Year	Last Year

b.　　　　　　　　　　MODERN BUILDING SUPPPLY

	This Year	Last Year

3.

Name _____

1. a.

	This Year	Last Year

b.

c.

d.

e.

f.

	This Year	Last Year
2. a.		
b.		

c. _____

3. _____

Problem 18-11

1.

	Method A	Method B	Method C	

2.

3.

Problem 18-12

Name _____

1. a.

b.

c.

2.

Transaction	The Effect on		
	Working Capital	Current Ratio	Acid-Test Ratio

Problem 18-13

Name _____

Problem 18-14

Problem 18-15   Name _____

1. a. and b.

	This Year	Last Year

Problem 18-15 (Continued) Name ______________________

2. a. – f.

	This Year	Last Year

Name _____

3. a. – g.

	This Year	Last Year

4.

Name _____

1.   HEDRICK COMPANY

	This Year	Last Year

HEDRICK COMPANY

	This Year	Last Year

3.

Problem 18-17   Name _____

1. a. – f.

	19x2	19x1

2.a. and b.

	19x2	19x1

c.

3.

1. a. – g.

	19x2	19x1

2.

3.

Name _____

1.

	19x2	19x1
Income Statement:		
Balance Sheet:	19x2	19x1

2.

TANNER COMPANY

		Key to Computation

TANNER COMPANY

		Key to Computation

Problem 18-20 (Continued)

Name _____

Computation of missing amounts:

Problem 18-20 (Continued)

Name _____

Computation of missing amounts:

Problem A-6   Name _____

1. a. and b.

2.

3.

	Repairs		Parts: Material Loading Charge	
	Total	Per Hour	Total	Percent

Problem A-7 _____ Name

1. a.

b.

c.

Problem A-7 (Continued)   Name _____

2 a. Supporting computations:

b.

c.

3.

Problem A-8

Name _____

1.

2.

3.

6.

7.

8.

Problem A-9

1. Supporting computations:

2. a.

  b.

  c.

3. a. Supporting computations:

b.

c.